May. 2013

WITHDRAWN

GEMS
NATURE'S JEWELS
DIAMONDS

By Eric Ethan

Gareth Stevens
Publishing

Please visit our Web site, www.garethstevens.com. For a free color catalog of all our high-quality books, call toll free 1-800-542-2595 or fax 1-877-542-2596.

For Michelle, a real gem.

Library of Congress Cataloging-in-Publication Data

Ethan, Eric.
Diamonds / Eric Ethan.
    p. cm. — (Gems, nature's jewels)
Includes index.
ISBN 978-1-4339-4716-2 (pbk.)
ISBN 978-1-4339-4717-9 (6-pack)
ISBN 978-1-4339-4715-5 (lib. bdg.)
1. Diamonds—Juvenile literature. 2. Mineralogy—Juvenile literature. I. Title.
QE393.E84 2012
553.8'2—dc22
                              2010032894

First Edition

Published in 2012 by
Gareth Stevens Publishing
111 East 14th Street, Suite 349
New York, NY 10003

Copyright © 2012 Gareth Stevens Publishing

Designer: Haley W. Harasymiw
Editor: Greg Roza

Photo credits: Cover, pp. 1, 5, 7, 8, 19, 21 Shutterstock.com; p. 9 Harry Taylor/Dorling Kindersley/Getty Images; p. 11 Patrick Landmann/Getty Images; p. 13 Per-Anders Pettersson/Getty Images; pp. 15, 17 Jonathan Torgovnik/Getty Images.

Printed in the United States of America

CPSIA compliance information: Batch #CS11GS: For further information contact Gareth Stevens, New York, New York at 1-800-542-2595.

CONTENTS

Words in the glossary appear in **bold** type the first time they are used in the text.

What Are Diamonds?

A diamond is a **transparent** gemstone that forms deep inside the earth. Diamonds are the crystal form of the element carbon. Carbon is one of the most common elements in the world. There's a lot of carbon on Earth, but only a small amount forms diamonds.

Diamonds form when carbon is under high heat and **pressure** for a long time. Diamonds found today formed 1 to 3 billion years ago.

GEM JOURNAL

Coal is also made of carbon. However, it forms closer to Earth's surface than diamonds do. There's not enough heat and pressure near the surface to turn carbon into diamonds.

Diamond is the most popular gemstone in the world.

Where Are Diamonds Found?

Diamonds are found in many parts of the world. The most important sources of gem-**quality** diamonds have long been central and southern Africa. Long ago, **volcanoes** carried diamond crystals up near the surface there. The diamond crystals mixed with a soft blue rock called kimberlite.

In 1870, word spread that diamonds had been found near Kimberley in the country of South Africa. Miners flocked to the area. In 43 years, miners found about 6,000 pounds (2,722 kg) of diamonds!

GEM JOURNAL

Diamond mining near Kimberley, South Africa, ended in 1914. An empty mine known as the Big Hole remains. It's 702 feet (214 m) deep!

This is a picture of the Big Hole in South Africa where diamond mining began in 1870.

What Do Diamonds Look Like?

Diamond is the hardest gemstone in the world. Raw diamonds form as transparent, eight-sided crystals. Once diamond crystals are cut and **polished**, they sparkle when light hits them. This makes them perfect for use in **jewelry**.

This raw, eight-sided diamond crystal was mined in Kimberley, South Africa.

8

Colored diamonds like these uncut crystals are very rare. ▼

Most diamonds are colorless. However, some are blue, green, red, yellow, or purple. They're called "fancy" diamonds, and they're very rare. Some colored diamonds form when small traces of other elements mix with the carbon. For example, blue diamonds contain boron.

Finding a Gem

Diamonds form deep inside Earth. They're brought to the surface in liquid rock. When this liquid rock cools and hardens, it forms kimberlite. The diamonds become trapped in the kimberlite. When miners find a kimberlite **deposit**, they dig into the earth and follow its path downward. They hope to find diamonds.

It takes a lot of people using big machines to find diamonds. Miners remove a pile of rock and dirt the size of a house to find just a few diamonds.

GEM JOURNAL

The tube in the center of a volcano is sometimes called a pipe. This is why kimberlite deposits, which used to be liquid rock inside a volcano, are often called "kimberlite pipes."

Diamond miners in South Africa use a heavy drill to make holes in the kimberlite. ▲

Open-Pit Mining

Diamond miners start by digging a hole straight down into a kimberlite deposit. Kimberlite mines are usually wide at the top, but become narrower the farther down they go. The result is a wide, bowl-shaped hole called an open-pit mine. Miners follow the kimberlite pipe until they stop finding diamonds.

Miners use big machines to break up the kimberlite rock in the mine. The rock is then put into trucks that take it out of the mine to be sorted.

GEM JOURNAL

When miners find a pocket rich in diamonds, they may dig narrow tunnels called shafts straight down into the kimberlite.

The Orapa diamond mine in the country of Botswana is the largest open-pit mine in the world.

Making Diamond Jewelry

A jeweler must be very careful when working with a diamond. Diamonds are very hard, but they're also **brittle**. A hard blow can easily crack a diamond.

A jeweler called a lapidary carefully studies a diamond before cutting. The jeweler looks for flaws to cut away from the diamond to make it stronger. The lapidary also decides what shape a diamond should be. Diamonds are cut into a basic shape using a diamond-tipped saw and lots of water.

GEM JOURNAL

Finished diamonds come in many shapes. These include round, oval, square, rectangular, pear shaped, and even heart shaped.

A lapidary carefully studies a large diamond crystal before cutting and polishing it.

What Are Facets?

After a diamond is cut into a basic shape, the lapidary **grinds** facets onto it. Facets are flat sides that allow the diamond to sparkle in light.

Faceted diamonds have been made for a very long time. Lapidaries have learned exactly where to put facets on a diamond crystal to make the finished gem look its best. It takes a lapidary a long time to learn where to put all the facets on a diamond and how to do it well.

Lapidaries carefully check their work as
they slowly add facets to diamonds with
a grinding wheel.

Valuable Diamonds

Diamonds are graded based on color, **clarity**, cut, and carat weight. The best diamonds are completely colorless. Cloudy or slightly yellow diamonds aren't as highly valued. Naturally colored diamonds are very rare, so they're very valuable. Flaws reduce a finished diamond's clarity and make it less valuable. The cut of a diamond is the one thing that a jeweler can control. When all the facets are cut in the right places, a diamond will sparkle brightly.

GEM JOURNAL

Gems are weighed using a unit called a carat. One carat is equal to 200 milligrams, or 0.007 ounce.

This is a collection of finished diamonds. ▲
Notice all the different ways diamonds
can be cut.

19

Really Rare Diamonds

In 1905, miners in South Africa found the largest diamond crystal ever mined. It weighed 3,106 carats! The nine largest gems made from the crystal were made into royal objects in the Crown Jewels of the United Kingdom. The largest—the Star of Africa—is the second-largest cut diamond in the world. It weighs over 530 carats!

The largest cut diamond in the world is a yellow-brown gem called the Golden Jubilee diamond. It weighs more than 545 carats!

Digging for Diamonds

- Diamonds were first mined in India about 6,000 years ago.

- Diamond is the birthstone for the month of April.

- Diamonds are so strong that they're used to cut and shape other gems.

- The only thing that can scratch a diamond is another diamond.

- About 80 percent of the diamonds mined every year are used to make cutting, grinding, and polishing tools.

- Man-made diamonds can be grown in just a few days.

- More man-made diamonds are sold each year than diamonds found in nature.

- Some people think the Hope diamond is cursed! No one wanted to buy it from its owner, so he gave it to the Smithsonian Institution in Washington, D.C.

Glossary

brittle: likely to break or crack

clarity: the state of being clear

deposit: an amount of a mineral in the ground that built up over a period of time

grind: to shape or smooth something with a rough surface

jewelry: pieces of metal, often holding gems, that are worn on the body

polish: to make something smooth and shiny by rubbing it with a soft cloth

pressure: a force that pushes on something else

quality: the standard or grade of something

transparent: letting light shine through

volcano: an opening in the ground that can shoot out hot, liquid rock

For More Information

Books

Petersen, Christine. *Groovy Gems*. Edina, MN: ABDO Publishing, 2010.

Symes, R. F., and R. R. Harding. *Crystal and Gem*. New York, NY: DK Publishing, 2007.

Web Sites

The Dynamic Earth
www.mnh.si.edu/earth/text/
Explore gems, minerals, and mining at the National Museum of Natural History Web site.

The Mineral and Gemstone Kingdom
www.minerals.net
Read about gems and minerals.

Index